Disturbing
the
Light

Titles by Samuel Green

Gillnets
Wind
Hands Learning to Work
Vertebrae
Keeping Faith
Communion
Vertebrae: Poems 1978-1994
Working in the Dark
The Only Time We Have
The Grace of Necessity
First Up: Barnstorming for Poetry
All That Might Be Done
Disturbing the Light

Disturbing
the
Light

Samuel Green

Carnegie Mellon University Press
Pittsburgh 2020

Acknowledgments

The author is grateful to the editors of the journals and anthologies in which some of the poems in this book first appeared, sometimes in slightly different versions:

Alaska Quarterly Review: "Dowser"; *American Life in Poetry*: "Butterflies"; *Best American Poetry, 2020*: "On Patmos, Kneeling in the Panagia"; *Cascadia*: "Falcon Watching, Point Disney" and "Elk"; *Clover*: "Wife Descending a Spiral Staircase," "Black Walnut," "Boot Jack," "Epitaph," "Four Portraits," "Slugs," "Talisman," "Skeleton," "Flood Tide," and "Barking Chipmunks"; *Green Linden Review*: "Barn Cat" and "Barred Owl"; *Limberlost Review*: "Unexploded Ordnance" and "Shoveling the Outhouse on Gary Snyder's Birthday"; *Poetry Daily*: "On Patmos, Kneeling in the Panagia"; *Poetry Ireland Review*: "Ditch Bouquet, Inis Mór"; *Poets Unite: The LitFuse @10 Anthology*: "Cat's Paw" and "Vocation"; *Prairie Schooner*: "Fishing," "On Patmos, Kneeling in the Panagia," "Street Vendor, Vung Tau, 1969," "Butchering Day," "What We Do with a Maul" and "Hoeing Beets, 1964, Skagit Valley"; *Terrain*: "Peavey, Mitchell's Boom, 1953" and "Anna's"; *WA 129*: "Belle de Boskoop"; *Washington State Museum of History*: "Net Needle"

The author wishes to thank the National Endowment for the Arts for a Fellowship in Poetry; Artist Trust of Washington for a Fellowship in Literature; James J. McAuley, who published a book when one was most needed; Stephen Sundborg, Andrew Tadie, Jason Wirth, Edwin Weihe, dear colleagues at Seattle University; Jerry and Kathy Willins, friends who have become like family; administrators and teachers connected with the Skagit River Poetry Project; the La Conner Rotary Club; Gerald Costanzo, Cynthia Lamb and Connie Amoroso at Carnegie Mellon University Press; island neighbors, living and gone; the Nelson Bentley tribe, especially: Sean Bentley, David Brewster, Marc Hudson, John Malek, Melinda Mueller, Anne Pitkin, Sherry Rind, Ann Spiers. Thanks also to the following for crucial advice and/or continuing encouragement: Wendell Berry, Tony Curtis, Michael Daley, Theo Dorgan, Dana Gioia, Donald Hall, Edward Harkness, Alicia Hokanson, Paul Hunter, Ted Kooser, Morten Lauridsen, David Lee, Sean McDowell, Wesley McNair, Tim McNulty, Paula Meehan, William O'Daly, Joseph Powell, Bill Ransom, Rachel Rose, Laurel Rust, Gary Snyder, Kim Stafford, Barry Sternlieb, Gary Thompson and Jeremy Voigt.

To my wife, Sally, the debt remains incalculable. Our granddaughter, Cora, is a bright, reliable star in the sky by which we navigate.

Cover illustration, *Raptor*, by Philip McCracken. Used by permission of the artist and Tim Bruce.

Book design by Martina Rethman

for Philip & Anne McCracken

&

in memoriam

Kim-An Lieberman,
Madeline DeFrees, Joan Swift,
Joan Stone, Lonny Kaneko, Stephen Clark, Keith Abbott,
Donald Hall, Mark Halperin, Joseph Duemer, Sam Hamill,
Frank Maloney, David Budbill, Marie Ponsot, Patrick Lane,
Tom Jay, Judith Roche, Dermot Healy, Eavan Boland,
Kurt Thorson, Michael Turnsen,
QMCM Leon K. First

&

James F. Sinclair, Jr.,1948-2011,
best friend, best man

Contents

I. Signaling

II. Outward Marks

III. Meat on the Bone

IV. Luminous Things

Before he died, he thought,
he might let someone know
how his own life felt.

—Philip Booth

I. Signaling

*. . . things which can be forgotten
but must first be told.*

—Les Murray

On Patmos, Kneeling in the Panagia

we hear the sound of a woman's high-heeled
    shoes striking the stones of the floor,
confident stride, strong hips, & I am
    back in a hospital bed at Clark Air

Force Base, the Philippines, September,
    1969, hearing a pair of shoes tapping their way
down the corridor outside my ward. I'd been
    knocked off a motorcycle by a drunk jitney

driver in Cavite City five days before,
    left leg shattered, compound fractures,
bone left on the street, flown to the surgeons
    at Clark who cleaned, debrided, sutured

& hung me up in traction. There were three
    of us in the ward. An air force guy
had blown the fingers off his left hand with a
    homemade bomb. He'd been at Cam Ranh Bay

at a party on the beach. Stupid, stupid, he said.
    The other guy was army, only seventeen,
right leg gone below the knee, left arm
    just above the elbow. Out on a routine

patrol his first week in-country, stood up to pee
    & the other newbie, pulling first guard,
shot him. They'd gone through boot together. He spent
    his days with a model ship, awkward

as it was to snap the pieces off & glue them into
    place one-handed. If I can do this, maybe
I can put myself together again, he said. Each night
    after lights out, he cried for an hour, softly,

into the snot on his pillow. The staff shrink was pissed
    I wouldn't say yes to amputation, said
I was immature. By that time I was hooked
    on Demerol, my butt cheeks already bared

at the stroke of each third hour, ready
    for the needle. End of that week,
late, they wheeled in three gurneys, jammed
    them tight against the walls, woke

us up. One held an army captain, left leg just
    a stump. He was hyper. Twitchy. Talked
a nurse into a telephone, called his wife. I'm fine,
    sweetheart, just fine. I'm coming home. Voice cracked.

He didn't mention the leg. Second guy was nothing
    but plaster & gauze, both arms in casts, slits
at eyes & mouth. He didn't move, didn't make
    a noise. Third man didn't have any sheets

over him, only a gown. Both legs gone, left arm missing
    nearly to the shoulder, rubber tubes in both
nostrils, a pair of IV bags hung on posts
    from either side of the gurney. His mouth

was open, eyes glazed. He made a sound like a pair
    of house slippers shuffling across a bare
carpet. His catheter bag was half full.
    One of the volunteers came in the door

just as the orderlies left. They were officers' wives
    for the most part, helping out while their
husbands flew supply runs or medevacs, stabilized
    patients, wrote long, exacting reports. The war

was far away, except for the wards. They fetched us
        decks of cards, looked for paperbacks,
helped us fill out daily menus, poured out
        cups of water, let us flirt a bit, ignored our looks

of lust. This one looked tired. She talked with
        the captain, who still seemed buzzed, his hands
fluttering like bats. His stump thumped up
        & down as he talked. His top sheet was stained

brown. He kept repeating home, home, home. I heard her
        say the plane would load & leave real early, he
should try to sleep. She put a hand on his
        forehead. He settled, closed his eyes. She

moved on to the gauze man, but didn't do much
        more than stand. She reached a hand as though
to touch, but stopped, adjusted the edge of a sheet
        & turned away. She murmured something low

to the third soldier, put her ear down near
        his face & nodded. She took a cup of ice
from a stand, carefully placed a chip between
        his lips & let it melt. She did it twice

more. Anything I can get you, soldier? Her voice
        was soft. He made a groan, like
a rusted nut coming loose on a bolt. Yeah,
        he said, I want some cake, a chocolate cake.

She watched as water dribbled down his neck, said
        What? He said it again. She shook her head.
I'm sorry, she said, but you can't eat. She tried to give him
        one more piece of ice. Lady, he said,

Jesus, lady, I don't wanna eat it. I just wanna look
    at it. He clamped his teeth down hard
grinding away at pain, turned his head to
    the wall. A minute more, she left the ward,

gone for the night. Then it was another shot
    for me, lights out again & sleep. They came
before breakfast, the nurses, changing linen,
    bags, IVs, a single bedpan. The same

orderlies took the captain first. He waved
    at us when he left. Then they took the white
ghost who never moved or spoke. That was when
    we heard the click of high heels out

in the hall & the volunteer walked in, dressed
    for a date, shimmering green gown,
blond hair hanging over bare shoulders. She was
    carrying a cake in two hands, a big round

three-layer cake, a single candle lit. She walked to
    the soldier's gurney & stopped. He heard
her coming & turned to look, the froth of chocolate
    same color as his skin. They didn't say a word.

The orderlies returned. One checked the blood
    pressure in his remaining arm; one
changed the flow on both IVs. The soldier
    raised the stump of his arm, let it down

soft on the rumpled sheet. His nose & eyes
    were leaking. The orderlies released
the gurney's brake & wheeled him out. She took
    a few steps back to let them pass.

We saw her shoulders shake. She stayed like that
   a long, long time, then turned & stepped
away in silence. The candle had burned out,
   left a trail of smoke, like a fighter jet

leaves across a clear sky. The guy who blew off
   his own hand said, She could have left some for us.
But it was all right. We couldn't have eaten
   the smallest bite of that darkness,

as here, on a Greek Island thousands of miles
   & more than forty years away,
I wait for the bread of the body, kneeling
   beside a woman who feeds me every day.

Street Vendor, Vung Tau, 1969

Eating is a small, good thing in a time like this . . .
—Raymond Carver

We pick him partly because there's a little
shade, partly because he meets our eyes
without a beggar's look, & partly because
he's handy, set up between two bars

that serve the local beer called 33, of which we've
drunk too many in both. Two boards across his cart make
a table braced by three deep bamboo baskets crammed
with produce & a fourth one filled with fresh-baked

bread, long brown baguettes. We order *banh mi,*
the sandwich of the street. The boy is maybe 15, so thin
he's lost in a short-sleeved white shirt too big for him, black
cotton trousers belted tight, rubber sandals. His shirt has been

mended by someone patient with a needle, fine stitches
fixing a rip above the right pocket like my grandmother knows
how to make. A little girl squats against the wall behind him
scribbling on a tablet with a pencil. Her pink tongue shows

at the edge of her mouth. He pulls a baguette
from the basket to his right, gracefully cuts
it in half, then slices each piece with a homemade
knife, the tip blunted like a sailor's rigging blade. It's

said each vendor has a private recipe for *banh mi,*
beginning with the base. This one starts with a sauce—
garlic mixed with spices, a splash of soy, chopped
chilies—basted on both faces of bread with a brush.

From a jar he shakes out pickled cucumber. Then thick leaves
of lettuce, shredded carrot. He slices both red & green

peppers into rings spread all along the length. In a few minutes
he will wrap the sandwiches in newsprint stained

with oil. We will pay him four times the price
in piasters, all our loose change & a couple dollar bills,
so that he will bow. To keep my sister with the nuns, he'll say.
We will step back into the random slap & jostle

of the street, the dance of the sidewalk, ranks
of parked Vespas & Hondas, the stalls with their stench
of hot briquettes, marinated meats mingled with exhaust,
piss & vomit in the doorways from which

we hear that time is on our side, how good it is
to be a Nashville rebel in the Monaco, the Star
Light, the US Moon or Olympia bars. We will wave
at girls in short leather skirts, smile at a pair

of shy twins in *ao dais*, one peach-colored, one
light blue. We are on leave from the war
for the day, sailors in civvies who want to be
normal. In just a few blocks we will hear

a sound like a full sea bag tumbling down a ship's
ladder, a soldier in cammies with one leg torqued
on the bottom step of an outdoor staircase, the other
flopped at a wrong angle on the sidewalk, a dark

pool spreading beneath his gashed neck. On the landing
above, an angry woman in a ripped silk blouse
will be shouting in French. We'll drop our food
on the street, kneel beside him. I will reach for a pulse

but get pushed aside by two off-duty corpsmen
who will shake their heads. Nothing. There will be

nothing. We will catch the first jeep headed toward our ship,
keep the story to ourselves. But here, right now, we

know none of this. There is only a boy for whom the war
means how to keep his little sister in school, make
his clothes last, find enough clean water for family
& garden & work for those slender hands that take

a fat red tomato from a basket & slice it with a knife
whose blade is sharp enough to cut away anything bad,
the fierce pride in his eyes as he puts our money in a box, then
wipes the boards clean, the rich juices looking nothing like blood.

Signaling

QMCM Leon K. First, USCG, 1929-2016

You taught me the first
longs & shorts of Morse
using a flashlight from the ship's
bow while I unhooded
the light on the flying
bridge & beat out the letters
with my right hand. Then
semaphore, which my father
learned in Scouts but forgot,
arms like the dials of an odd clock
spelling out the alphabet.

Flag hoists were easy enough,
codes we copied from the book: Quebec
for "Quarantine"; Oscar for "Man
Overboard." We read a flag signal
on the practice mast right to left, top
to bottom, same way a poem
is read in Chinese.

Two years later, standing
watch in Vietnam, I saw
a gunner on the shore tower
tracking targets floating down
a river on salvaged boards,
scrambled up to the bridge,
spelled out: *Hold fire. Kids*
diving for pennies. They were so close
to the kill zone. I damaged my eyes
reading code at max distance all
along the coast from Cua Viet
to An Thoi, terrified I might get
something wrong, get someone

killed. I still walk the beach
sometimes at night here
on our island, sit on a drift log
& flash *C-Q, C-Q,* "any receiver,"
wanting to connect. The day I heard
you died I thought of you there
in Michigan, deep into Alzheimer's,
your fingers maybe tapping
out letters on your bedsheet—
military corners, squared away
& tight enough to bounce
a quarter off—no one
receiving. *Z-W-C,* " just between
operators," I rapped on my desk,
T-K-S, Chief, then *K,*
"invitation to transmit."
I imagined your answer
from the other side
of the bar, each dot
& dash exact & bright: *S-T-A-R,*
"Shit, That's All Right."

Unexploded Ordnance

for Mona Lydon-Rochelle

> *We must learn to live with bombs*
> *Shaking the sky*
> *And the heavy smell of gunpowder . . .*
> —Duc Thanh, Soldier Poet

We grew up on the March of Dimes, the president's face
on a ten-cent piece, the threat of polio real as the braces
on a classmate's legs, the cost of a carton of milk.

My mother pasted Easter Seals on cards
& letters, bought red paper poppies outside
the supermarket door. On white cane days

we threw our pennies into buckets for the blind,
for the bell-ringers at Christmas, brought canned
food to school for the holiday poor.

1.
My father's mother sold her extra milk & butter,
eggs, old hens for the pot. She kept her
coins in baskets or empty Folgers cans. Each
month she made a count & set aside a share
for Father Flanagan's boys. Another
portion went to needy kids in Ecuador.
A neighbor helped her buy the money orders.
It wasn't that she practiced what she preached,
because she wouldn't preach to anyone.
There was a Boys Town calendar on the wall
beside her phone. Photos of María, Rosa, Juan
arrived in letters with exotic stamps on frail
paper. For herself, she made do, got by
with little. If asked, she'd say she was just fine. OK.

2.
It's nineteen sixty-nine, the DMZ
at Cua Viet, & I am knocked to the deck
of my ship's signal bridge by shock
waves from the battleship *New Jersey*,
half her guns engaged & sending shells
in-country more than twenty miles
to cool down a landing zone, stop
an enemy mortar team, maybe keep
a recon squad alive. Not one man
on a gun crew would think about
a live round waiting in the dirt
for more than forty years. And me? My hand
dropped a hundred grenades over the ship's side
into the river at Cat Lo. They didn't all explode.

3.
In Quang Tri the school kids study a new
three Rs. *Recognize,* they chant,
& run through the roster of UXOs: "bombies,"
mortars & mines, artillery shells, grenades,
old ammo. They learn to read shapes, what hides
in rust, a pile of stones or the laced roots of trees.
Retreat, they say, meaning go back, don't
touch, watch each foot, don't squat to view
it closer. The weight of a spider could set
it off. Just call their friends & go, get
an adult & *Report,* tell someone, right now,
what doesn't add up. They already need to know
the ways of thirty-seven poisonous snakes,
as well. Their daily world is a dangerous place.

4.
Cluster shells are the worst. They came
in metal pods that opened in the air,

six hundred metal spheres the size
of softballs, each a separate bomb
designed to rupture, pierce, shred, tear
up anything soft, whatever grew, grazed,
flew, crawled, ran or simply stopped
in place. Sometimes when they dropped
they didn't open, buried themselves deep
in the ground, got caught up on limbs
or smothered under elephant grass, became
a nest of metal lumps, corroded, fused in a heap
you might pass safely year by year by year,
until—one lightest step—they do what they were made for.

5.
Yes, there was a loan arranged by Commune Worker
Nhi to buy two pigs for Mrs. Thi, whose leg a mine
blew off, whose husband died, whose only daughter
had to work, whose two grandkids can finally go
to school. And yes, it's true that Dang Van Han,
who nicked the skin of a mine in his field with a hoe,
can tend his crops of peanuts & peppers with much less
hurt. Ms. Nhi set him up with a surgeon. And, yes,
it's a fact that now Le Huong has two cows to help support
his family, new skills to manage pain from yet
another hidden mine. But, listen, this is also true:
young Le Quynh Nhi was first to sit with a cup of tea
steeped from lemongrass & say, *I want to hear you
share your story. Sister, Brother, there is time. Tell me.*

6.
Simon tells his late-night AA group he thought
he saw his best friend waiting for a red light
to change, & a charge went off in his own chest:
fifty years, but his buddy Lee from boot was still a kid,
eighteen, eyes full of boogie, restless

fingers tapping the steering wheel, head
shaking a little to a beat—some sixties tune,
no doubt—as though he hadn't put his big foot down
on a homemade mine, right leg off above the knee;
as though the corpsman stopped the blood & Lee
was on a chopper *di di mau* & safe. Because there he
was, rolling down the window of a cherry-
red Chevy, lobbing change toward the paper plate
on which Simon had scrawled: *Please Help a Vet.*

The same small village blacksmith who takes the steel
shards of shells & bombs to forge a hoe or batter out
a cowbell in a shower of sparks on a homemade anvil,

can also conjure a monk's begging bowl. It takes eight
strips of scrap steel cut & pounded together with heat,
a copper & herb paste melted to seal the seams, twenty

thousand hammer blows for the final shape. Imagine it
done, held before the poorest of the poor in silent asking,
& how a single grain of rice might make the metal ring.

II. Outward Marks

All I want is a door into the dark.

—Seamus Heaney

Inclinations

for Frank & Hazel Green

My grandfather loved the steady pulse of a diesel,
the straight wake of a boat.

My grandmother preferred the sound
of a hummingbird working the long flutes
of honeysuckle.

My grandfather loved the smell of fish
in the hold, on the decks, in the clothes
he wore for a week at a time.

My grandmother preferred the light
odor of hay in the barn, fresh milk in the pail,
dried dung on the tails of her cows.

My grandfather loved the taste of a charred
steak, reheated gravy, whiskey on the tongue,
in the throat, the burn in the belly.

My grandmother preferred homemade jelly
on homemade bread, a bowl of berries & cream
from her own cows, cool water from the well.

My grandfather loved the touch of smooth new paint
on a barn wall, the scratch & itch of hay
in his overalls after filling the loft.

My grandmother preferred the soft hair
on a calf's flank, the feel of fresh oats sliding
through her fingers as she filled the grain boxes.

My grandfather chose the slow waltz
of cancer to take him out, a lifetime
of cigars & cigarettes. He took his meals

from a blender poured into a tube.
My grandmother preferred the quick jig
of a stroke, gone in days.

Neither of them wanted to be
any bother. Their ashes were scattered
by their grandson far from each other.

Barking Chipmunks

was simple enough in theory. My father talked me
through it. The idea was to put a high-powered
bullet between the bark a chipmunk clung to

& the slick sapwood, then rescue it, stunned,
from the ground. The fall, he said, would hurt it
not a bit. I imagined it tame & perched

on my shoulder, nattering, nibbling my ear
with affection. I'd built a cage already: scrap-wood
frame, wire mesh from an old crab pot. We used

the 30/40 Krag, a carbine, something
from the Spanish-American War just sixty years
behind. It was my father's favorite gun. At ten,

I'd cleaned it a hundred times. We drove
to a patch of woods on state-owned land,
second-growth, logged a long time back. It took

a minute to hear the chatter of a chipmunk,
find it maybe fifty feet up the trunk of a Douglas
fir. I pressed my cheek against the stock, snicked off

the safety with my thumb & aimed exactly where
my father said, right behind the claws where bark
was thickest. My breath was halfway out

when the rifle kicked. It took a good
fifteen minutes to find the chipmunk
dead, a bloody smear of fur & shredded

bark. My father said we'd try again.
I shook my head. My shoulder
hurt. I thought it should.

Fishing

Mural, Anacortes Post Office, created for the Treasury
Department's Section of Fine Arts by Kenneth Callahan, 1940

My father is squinting up at the mural
    at my request, looking bent & small
in his eighties. He fished with his own
    father when young & knew boats. This one,
a seiner, takes up the whole left foreground,

bow & most of the hull out of frame, showing
    the white pilot house & everything aft:
the working deck with a wide open hatch
    & the space in which the close dance of nets
gets acted out, cork floats, lead weights,

the hundreds of feet of stiff cotton line with its
    intricate knots. To the right is the seine skiff,
just beginning the routine of making a set.
    What my father is amazed at right off
is how many are in the crew: nine visible men,

twice what his father hired each season. There
    are four in the stern sending the net over
the gunwale, a fifth at the hatch. There are
    two in the skiff: one at the oars, another
to manage that end of the web being fed

from one boat to the other. Two more men
    are barely in-frame on the left, one
in a second skiff next to the hull, another
    leaning toward him, both hands on the rail.
We can't tell what they're up to. All

of them wear foul weather gear, rubber boots,
    slickers or wool coats, waterproof hats. As a boy

I stood with my mother in a long line to buy
        stamps, staring up at those men who were just
like my grandfather's friends, the ones who'd hoist

me up like a fresh-caught salmon when the nets
        were laid out on the dock. They said I was too small
to keep & threatened to throw me back, dangling me out
        over the water. I was afraid of their heavy smell
like a tidal stink, their rough talk. Holding

my mother's hand, I imagined my father
        disappeared into water dark as the colors
in the painting. I wanted to be good
        so he'd come back to us, & each time he did
I believed I'd rescued him. Now he is caught

in the slow, steady current of dementia,
        & there's nothing anyone can do to bring him
about. The nets of his memory have rips
        that won't be mended, & thoughts slip
through in flashes of silver. It was always a numb

act of faith, fishing, risking one's life & no
        guarantee what would come wriggling over
the side, more dogfish than salmon some years, more
        tears in the nets & days at the pier for repairs.
So many men on the crew, my father says

again. Four on the nets, two in the skiff, two
        more doing god-knows-what. *There's another:*
someone's got to be on the wheel, my father
        says. *Some old guy you hope to hell might know*
what he's at. And that last man, the odd one apart

looking down into the open hatch, shoulders
    hunched, head bowed, hands meeting nearly
at his knees in a gesture that could be purely
    weariness, resignation, thanks, or prayers.
That one, Father, could be me. I was always yours.

Four Portraits

I. Mother, Frying Bacon & Eggs

She is stirring curls of fat with a fork in a cast-
iron skillet black as her mood. Hot grease
spatters her wrist. She doesn't flinch.
The curlers in her hair are loose.
She won't look at my father, waiting in his place
at the table. Smoke from her Camel swirls
above the pan. Ash falls among the cracklings. Coffee
cools on the counter beside her. Her children are still
in bed. Already she is dreading the dishes
they will dirty. Already she is feeling dry
as the meat she parcels onto a plate. My father likes
the yolk in his eggs unbroken. This morning
she will serve them scrambled across
the dry toast of their life.

II. Father, Oiling His Work Boots

He keeps his eyes cast
down the whole time, tin of grease
balanced on his right knee. I saw him flinch
once at a gouge in the sole of his left boot, loose
threads unraveling, the saw marks close to the place
his toes shaped the leather. He is poor. Money swirls
away like rain in a gutter. He reheats coffee,
saves what he can, cares for his boots, his tools. He is still
a puzzle to his oldest son, someone who needs to dish
out the stale bread of advice based on the dry
crust of his own childhood. Still, that same son likes
this time with his father, these early morning
minutes when something quiet is possible between them. Across
his knees he is worrying his boots, his child, his life.

III. Grandfather, Sharpening His Pocketknife

Because he makes a mess, he likes to do it in a cast-
off kitchen chair on the front porch. He scrapes old grease
from the stone, adds a bit of oil & spit, doesn't flinch
when the blade slips, adds a bit of blood to the mix. His loose
overall bib makes a pad on his lap. I watch him place
the blade with care each time, then the quick, sure scrape, a swirl
at the edge as a flourish to finish the stroke. Brandy in his coffee
keeps his hand as steady as it gets, which is never entirely still.
He drops cups on the steps, drops dishes
on the concrete he poured for the stoop. When the stone is dry
he scrapes some hair from his wrist as a test. He likes
a sharp knife in his pocket, likes to slice his morning
sausage into thin dimes spread across
his eggs. Each day his blade wears thinner. Like his life.

IV. Grandmother, Picking Boysenberries

She's started on the west end of the row so she casts
no shadow on the fruit. What's ripe shines like grease
in the morning wet, a deep maroon. Her quick hands flinch
only once at a fat garter snake. She tugs it loose
from the berry canes, turns & finds a safe place
for it amid the thick leaves of the beans, a swirl
of brown among the green. She fills the old coffee
tin—Folgers—& empties it into a dishpan. She is still
for only a moment: there is laundry to sort, dishes
to scrape, mash to mix for the pigs & dry
corn to scatter for the hens. They can wait a bit. She likes
the ripening silence, lifts herself back into morning
& lets her stiff hands move again up & across
the row, working into the rising sun of her old life.

Flood Tide

Again the dream: my mother & I tucked
into the stern of the skiff, an old one,
lapstrake, leaking a little at two sprung
seams. My father, midships, is rowing
faster than we imagined
possible, white oars flapping
like the wings of a giant
frightened seabird
trying to launch himself
into the air away
from us & all danger.

Hoeing Beets, 1964, Skagit Valley

I think I will do nothing for a long time but listen . . .
—Whitman

What the farmer wants is plain.
He sharpened five hoes before dawn
on a wheel in the barn after fried oatmeal,
toast & eggs. He spends no time
with the names of weeds. Instead
he shows us what a beet leaf
looks like. Anything that isn't this,
he says, chop it out. Make it dead.
He hopes we wore practical shoes.

The four women run from nineteen
to thirty-five, three of them married.
What they want depends. Audrey hopes
to buy her daughter a bike. Linda's in love
with a sailor, owes her sister long
distance charges. Sheila hides vodka
away from her husband. Sue needs new
sheets for their bed, they're wearing
the bridal ones out.

What the gulls want is whatever we disturb
in this flood plain soil, beetles, grubs,
the wriggle & curl of worms. They follow
at our backs, a squalling storm of squawks & wing flaps.

Dust devils rise & spin beside us. A kitchen
screen door slams, then slams again. The farmer
bangs on something rusty with a wrench,
his arm halfway up before we hear the sound.

I am fifteen, standing in for my mother.
Anyone might guess what I think

I want: to watch the way these women
bend & reach, the slow stretch of fabric,
smell of their sweat, the way patches of skin

shine in the day's raunchy heat, how Audrey licks
the small fine hairs on her upper lip
after each swig from the red Kool-Aid jug,
how Linda plucks white threads from a rip
in her pink pedal pushers & winds them
round a thumb, how Sheila hums
a Patsy Cline tune, chopping weeds
on each stressed syllable falling to pieces
all down the half-mile rows, how Sue washes
her feet when we stop for lunch, lets me
dry them with the loose tail of my shirt.

They work heads down, chittering
like starlings, these women who are tired
of pinochle, tired of perms, tired
of opening cans. They are a sisterhood
of secrets, the uses & failings of men.
Their mothers are dealing with night
sweats, their grandmothers fret about rest
homes. They pretend to forget I am here,
the awkward boy at the neighborhood bus stop,
the one who plays cards with his mother
& friends, the one who can keep his mouth shut,
this boy they think of as shy. They know
what I believe I want, what I need, & why.

Belle de Boskoop

for Chris Stern, 1950-2006

We were back a day from saying good-bye
to an old friend. I stepped outside
to fetch wood for the fire & heard
what sounded like shots or the angry door
of a truck being slammed over & over—
tree branches snapping under eight to ten
inches of the weightiest snow
we'd seen in our lives, thousands breaking
across the island. We lost limbs
from every tree in the orchard: plums,
apples, fig, cherry. The peach tree bent
in a long arc to the grass. Only the Boskoop
couldn't carry the load & split
at its crotch, the trunk a white wound
clean to the frozen ground.

Named for some Dutch village
beauty two centuries gone, we bought it
for its later ripening, not so red
as William's Pride, not so good
in the cellar as Jonagold,
but sweetening with time.

While it snowed, our dear friend died.

When it thawed we used wood clamps
to force the trunk together, took an old tube
from a bicycle tire & stretched it round the bark
from grass to crotch, cut cedar braces to help bear
the load & called it good. Next summer we thinned
the fruit to lighten the weight. Clamps & tubing
came off in the fall. The scar was a jagged ridge
of bark, imperfect as our own healing
though we bore no outward mark.

Epitaph

for Hayduke

The hummers at the bleeding hearts,
the juncos in their bath,
the rats out in the compost bin,
young rabbits in the yard

are wary of the red-tailed hawk,
the silence of the owl,
but safer than they were before
we dug our old cat's grave.

Warnings

Here it comes, say the talking heads, &
It's big. Always the quick assumption it's
Going to be grave, & always the fearful reminder, the
High-water mark: Columbus Day, '62. We knew
Where we were, my wife & I, what we did, how bad
It got. Our fathers worried about the roof, our mothers
Nudged us away from windows. I was thinking about
Deer season, opening day next morning. So
What if two billion board feet of trees blew down?
All I wanted was my rifle, oiled & oiled again,
The knife in my belt I'd honed to an edge that
Could shave my arm with only a little spit, the fine
Hairs lifting onto the blade. No mention now
Of that storm in '21 my grandmother got
Caught out in, tree trunks four feet through snapping,
The crowns sailing off into darkness. She & her mother were
On their way home with horses & a new
Baby, got penned by spruce & cedar, hemlock, fir,
Each crossing each like spilled armloads of kindling, the
Rich scent of pitch thick as winter rain. They left the horses,
Found a way to the shake-sided house after dark. Loggers loved
It, lived on salvaged logs for a decade. No frightened horses
For us. We're hunkered down, lamps full of oil,
The stove hot, wood piled on the back porch, tarps over
Exposed tools. We've become elders. We know much about
Expecting the worst, like the dark winds of illness that we can
Never prepare for, no matter the storms we've weathered.

Butchering Day

It was my grandmother did the choosing,
because dry was dry, & all she was losing

was the heat of a body in the tie-up's
cold mornings. My father gave me a rope.

I followed the sound of her bell to the west
field where she grazed with the rest

of her sisters, nosing her way through a patch
of white clover & vetch. She let me fetch

her up, stood switching her tail at the flies
as I clipped the rope to her bell strap. Her nose

brushed my ear. I led her through the gate, across
the ditch & onto the county road—*Ho, Boss, come, Boss!*

Her hooves sounded strange on the gravel. My father
& two of his brothers waited at the long shed where

the seine nets were stored in the off-season.
An uncle held out the rifle for no special reason

except I was eight & a boy was a help or a boy
was a bother. They could send me to play

in the kitchen, or show me what they believed
a man's work was. I wanted to be brave,

so took the gun. The old cow blinked, flicked
her ears, chewed her cud, lifted her tail & shit

a green stream of pudding. Between the eyes, said
my father, so the white blaze on her head

was only a target to find, not a cow to kill,
& the old pump action .22 Special

not too heavy. I had to stand on a feedbox
to get the muzzle high enough. I fixed

on a point exactly between her horns & eyes
& squeezed the trigger. She slumped to her knees

like those animals in a Christmas manger,
then rolled on her right side. They lashed her

hind legs to a singletree, & used a block
& tackle to hoist her off the grass. When her neck

stretched out, my father stuck the long thin
blade in her throat & cut a clean line

from side to side while an uncle slid a milk bucket
under to catch the blood. He took a packet

of Luckies from a pocket & passed them out. I sat
on my box & thought about gravy, thought

about jars in the pantry, canned meat & broth, a full
freezer of steaks, roasts & ribs, hamburger, stew meat, all

wrapped in white paper. Her hide would come back
as leather. We'd eat the heart, the liver, the fat

kidneys. This was knife & saw work, too sharp a task
for a boy. The men took a snort from a flask

& sent me back to the house with the leather neck
belt & bell which clanged just once as I walked.

Peavey, Mitchell's Boom, 1953

What my father couldn't say
    is how he put together the sound
of the donkey engine starting up
    with the strain of cables biting
into bark & so understood that the new guy
    was dumping a truckload of logs
from the boom deck into the salt
    without checking whether anyone
was down below still rafting the strays
    from the prior load, which was,
in fact, what my father was doing,
    balanced on the butt of a red cedar
about to hook another with his pike
    pole, his cork boots giving enough
traction on the otherwise slick wood that he chucked
    his pole to one side & dove for the bottom,
praying the tide was high enough to keep
    the logs off him, but so scared when he hit mud
he tried to dig himself even deeper, squirming between
    two fat deadheads lying parallel
to one another in the black muck,
    frantically wishing he was part geoduck,
sinuses aching from the pressure, his left palm
    catching on the hook of a lost peavey buried
in the sludge, holding himself down with it
    while the logs above tore up the bright green
rug of the surface, some of them tumbling
    all the way to the bottom, but bouncing off
the sunken hemlocks on either side of him,
    so that only his right shoulder was bruised,
& he couldn't tell you how, though it felt like
    something with tentacles was squeezing his chest,
he was able to stay down long enough to wrench
    that peavey from the mud & haul it left-handed
through a shower of bark scraps up to a surface still

shuddering & heaving with logs, having no idea his
stubborn eldest son would break the handle
sixty-five years later while trying to roll a windfall
white fir & would order a new handle made of radiant
ash from the Joseph Peavey factory back in Maine,
because a good tool, by god, might some day save your ass
& is something you do not waste.

Net Needle

for Jerry Costanzo

When I was ten, Goody Matsen showed me
how to carve one. We sat on a pair of stools
on the cannery dock while my grandfather,
the skipper, fueled up his seiner. *Might as well*

do something useful while we wait. He kept
a box of blanks beneath his bunk,
sawed from a slab of yew he'd scrounged
off somebody's wood pile. *Hard*

wood, he said, *& tough, but it cuts good*
with a sharp knife. He had an old
Case Stockman, the spey blade honed
to the width of an awl for close-in

work. He let me use the Swedish Foster
he carried in a sheath on his belt:
Sharp enough to shave a four-day beard
after a three-day drunk. He liked

a needle about the length from his wrist
to the tip of his middle finger. *Plus*
a fat gnat's eyebrow, for luck. He said
it should be wide as a slice

of store-bought bacon, & thick
as two pieces before they're cooked.
He let me trace a pattern on the wood
with the chewed-up stub of a pencil,

but said I'd need to let my hands
remember the shape—crescent

on one end, tapered head on the other.
It looks a bit like a fish without

its fins, he said. The tongue for the twine
should be twice as long as the depth
of the notch in the tail, starting at the dorsal
& ending just in front of where the gills

would be. He told me to relax,
that short, even strokes, where the blade
lifts little curls, are better
than long, hard, deep ones that gouge

the grain. *You want the wood to sigh,*
not grunt. His own hands shook so much
he could only half fill his mug
from the thermos, but they stilled

when he gripped the knife. *Do*
what I do, he said. He roughed out two
in the hour the boat was gone.
We'll sand them later, so they'll slide real

easy against the nets. We can pour some coffee
into that skillet we fried the bacon in
for lunch & soak them overnight
to put some grease & color into

the wood. Tomorrow, he said, we'd work
on patching some webbing. *You make a tool,*
you ought to for Chrissake know how
to use it, & the next one should be

better. His boatwright brother
helped him carve his first. *Since I was hung*

over so much, Arnie said I ought to have a chore
to remind me I was worth the breakfast

I couldn't eat. 'There will always be holes
& tears in your life,' he said, 'always something falling
out, slipping away.' He hoped I might learn to save
what I could. Some days are okay. This one's been good.

Meditating Frog

Sculpture: fieldstone, by Philip McCracken, 1955

He is squatting like a Buddha on a rounded
rock, front arms tucked beneath the great bulge
of himself, two fingers on each hand touching,
rear toes splayed just short of the forward
curve. His head is tilted back, eyes closed
to slits. Light shimmers as on damp skin
in soft lamp glow. There is a slash
of mouth, a single line neither frown nor grin
but somewhere between, as though it's all one:
whether having swum through the thickest slime
on the bottom of pond or lake—the black muck
of rotted leaves, gray fur of fungus
on the bellies of dead fish, the slick snot
of egg sacks—or risen from mud to sit
on a fallen cattail stalk, lily pad, mass of duckweed
or convenient stone in the day's heat, cool rain,
moon or star shine, a feast of mosquitoes, dragonflies,
gnats, or empty air. The sac at his throat is stretched
tight as an Irish bagpipe's bladder. He could be just about
to call out everything he knows—dark song, light
song—or about to jump into the sound
of himself, entering the artist's unseen water.

Prayer Beads

for Paula Meehan & James J. McAuley

Not the bead, but the ball of the thumb
on the bead. Not the prayer, but the willing
act of prayer, another decade
of Hail Marys or the Heart Sutra—
Gate Gate Paragate Parasamgate
Bodhi Svaha—luminous or sorrowful
mysteries, & never mind whether
it's dried seeds strung together
on kitchen twine, carved wood, bone,
abalone shell, tiny balls of baked clay, or,
like these, hand-worked Mexican silver,
gift of a man who knew full well
what telling the beads might tell.

Talisman

for Phyllis Ennes, 1928-2013

If her father were here
with those hands that knew
how to coax stories
from wood, we'd ask him
to carve her in cedar
as *Raven Stealing the Sun*,
which he could then saw
into sections the size
of a greengrocer's thumb,
then fit them back together
with intricate joins, cunning
latches, so those who loved her
might take her apart,
each of us bearing the art
in a curve of wing, a small motif
of feather, a clear & clever
eye, a portion of beak,
until all that's left
is the brilliant berry of light
she brought us—
if her father hadn't gone
into darkness before her,
if she hadn't already
given herself away
one thoughtful offering
at a time.

Vocation

i.m. John O'Leary, Irish poet, 1954-2012

The morning he turned sixteen he slid
from his bed before dawn & hiked to the limestone
cliffs west of the village, past the beach where a boulder
was blessed into a boat that left its keel mark

gouged into rock when monks launched themselves
into the waves. He climbed down to an arch
that spanned a channel gouged deep
by the sea. He undressed in full view

of a cow, cud-chewing sheep, folded his clothes
neat as a mother, then stood on the stone edge
in his white skin, frightened, for half an hour.
It was cold. He was shaking. When the sun began rising

he held out his arms. By now he was breathing
with the pulse of the sea, the rush of waves washing
in from a hundred yards out, the break, then receding.
He stepped forward at the wave's height & fell

feet first, cruciform, forty feet. It hurt when he hit.
He wanted it to. Then the plunge into dark stopping
short of the bottom. There was, he said,
a sort of languid letting go before the slow lifting

toward light. When he broke forth into air he opened
his mouth even before taking a breath & spoke
from where he'd been, just as he would do
for the rest of his life.

III. Meat on the Bone

Ain't no matter you fill the plate,
it's how much meat's on the bone.

—Folk Saying

Otter

If you've ever seen
an otter swim, one
long, intelligent muscle,
supple as new rope,
how it moves like ink
caught in a current,
then you'd know
how wrong it feels
to see this one
loping in a panic
along the center
of a dirt road
a quarter mile
from the bay,
a heavy bag
of thick skin,
rear end humped
like the base of a clumsy S
tumbled on its side,
twisting at the neck
to watch our truck
looming behind
through the dust,
you'd maybe recall
that dream of something
large & dark coming
toward you down
the suddenly
unfamiliar road
of your life.

Dowser

for Fred Adams

We expected someone a bit exotic,
brooding, with a face like a lake
reflecting clouds. What we got
was a neighbor in green plaid
work shirt, faded ball cap

& patched jeans, who brought nothing
with him but a freshly honed knife,
with which he cut the crotch
of a young maple at our clearing's edge,
trimming until he had the stem

& arms of an upper case Y. It had to be
slim enough to flex, he said, it wouldn't bend
so much as twist. He gripped one arm
of the Y in each fist, thumbs toward his chest,
the slight curve of the stem pointing a little

up & out, & then meandered through
what would become our orchard
in a few more years, turning at the hips,
scribing an arc in the air north to south, until
the rod began to twitch & tugged itself down

at a clump of saw grass. He saw my look
of doubt, & offered to let me try,
kept one arm of the stick in his right
hand while I held the left, & backed up.
When we stepped forward, I willed it

not to bend, but though I fought to keep my fist
straight, I felt the bark break & the fibers
twist against my skin as the wand tugged

& wrenched itself down toward the grass
again. Our neighbor took out his knife,

sharpened the stem, & stuck it as a marker
into the grass. *You'll find good water*
at a hundred & twenty-eight feet. Doesn't matter
if you drill or not. It's there. He said there'd be no
charge & left to return to his chores, leaving us

to think how somewhere below
was an aquifer, a fickle lens of water,
how the driller charged by the foot,
dry well or wet, how all we had was
choice, & our unrelenting thirst.

Island Potluck

You might think we go
to the North Bay beach
or the one-room school,
or the edge of the field
near the Maypole
for the food, & we do
have an appetite for goat
meat curry, salmon grilled
over alder, tender greens
thinned from a garden
& rinsed in well water,
an old hen stewed in vinegar
on the back of a wood-fired range,
potatoes roasted with rosemary,
baked ling cod, boiled crab
for the cracking, homemade bread
with handmade cheese,
canning jars of cider, jugs
of blackberry wine. Or
we could be there for the music,
the neighbors who pull out
a fiddle, flute, penny whistle,
concertina, bass, guitar. Of course
we go for stories about the old ones
whose names flare at the edge
of conversation like sparks
rising from a campfire: Chuck,
Elaine, Jimmy, Mildred,
Ann. We all miss Dorothy's
deviled eggs. We come to find out
who's well, who's failing, who's falling
in or out of love, for what the young
in the shadows might learn
from their elders, quiet voices
in the driftwood, at the clearing's

edge, out by the school
swings. We bring bowls & serving
spoons, favorite pots & skillets,
a colorful sorting of plates,
& the empty cups of ourselves.

In the Tules

James Cowan, murdered 1868, Waldron Island

Nearly a hundred & fifty years ago, shot
& stuffed beneath a pile of brush. My dog knew
where. The men who found me followed him
from my shack, a goddamned turnip dangling
like a plumb bob from his mouth. They thought
he was a loyal friend to bring me food. The stew-
brained mutt just liked to dig them up. It was Skookum
Tom who killed me, but no one proved it. He hanged

for someone else's death. They say when
the frogs go suddenly silent in the reeds,
it means I'm restless. Only fretful thing is my mind
that won't forget a good cow I planned to breed
to my meanest bull. Their calf would have been
something special. My neighbors ate them when I died.

Shoveling the Outhouse
on Gary Snyder's Birthday

Light that shines on dung
is not part of the dung.
—Rumi

Because we pour our piss in the compost,
there's only the smell of must & damp
stove ash from a thousand fires. Everything

is dry. I built hinges into the floor,
so it lifts with only a little scraping. When light
angles in, spiders the size of a fingertip wake

from their daily practice & find whatever cracks
they can in the cedar shakes, or simply curl back
into themselves & wait. The shovel is an old one,

long-handled hickory slick with a coat
of linseed oil, the blade a little bright
at its tip. In two hours, ten wheelbarrows

of songbird phrases, owl calls, the smoky flourishes
of breath on frosted mornings, go to fill a bowl
in the ground near a rotted nurse log, shades

of brown, black & gray combed & leveled, nothing
like the patterns a monk might make with a *kumade*,
a wood-tined rake, no cloud patterns, no currents

of sea or wind-wiped lake. Star flowers there
next spring, heal-all, fringecup & another two years
of space to use & leave the self behind.

What We Do with a Maul

Go-devil, my grandmother called it, part axe,
    part sledge. These days some mauls are made
with fiberglass handles. They're harder
    to break or crack, but a good tough grade

of wood feels better. Something about the way
    a hand slides on hickory makes it your own.
Axe-eye or ox-eye doesn't seem to make much
    difference. A little linseed oil rubbed in

keeps the wood alive. Drive in soft metal
    wedges to hold the head tight. You need
at least a two-pound splitting wedge, not too sharp
    at the edge, tapered, long as a maul's head.

I paint mine orange. Too easy to lose one
    in brush. A pair is a good idea in case
the wood won't split. A second almost
    always gets the stuck one loose

enough to ease out. If it was spring cut, bucked
    & left to lie till fall, the round itself should tell
you where to put the wedge. There'll be checks
    on the face where it tried to pull

itself apart as it dried. Set the blade in a line
    with a crack, but off-center, out
toward the edge. Keep the first taps
    light, three or four whacks to get it set

so it doesn't jump free at the first hit. Make
    sure it doesn't line up with a knot. It's hard
to tell you how to stand. I like to swing from
    an angle, not straight on. You should be scared

enough to pay attention. The head of a wedge
    will mushroom over time & steel can chip
from the sides. You could lose an eye, break
    a tooth. Sometimes the wedge will leap

back up if the grain's too tight, as though the wood
    itself is throwing it back at you. There's a scar
on my left leg from that. Edges sharpen
    where the beaten metal tapers & tears

the skin of your fingers. Gloves help, but get
    a good pair, heavy leather, the cheap ones
wear out fast. Field hogs, white fir, hemlocks,
    wild cherry, & some of the pines

split hard. Doug fir, red alder, big leaf maple
    will fall apart with one or two good licks,
most times, especially green. It's a good idea
    to keep a hatchet close in case the wedge sticks

deep in one of those swerves the grain can take,
    & you need to hack it out. Keep it sharp,
kneel close, & take short strokes. Sometimes
    a chunk just will not come apart

without hurt to yourself or tools. Set them
    aside for the saw. No shame. I've cut & split
eight to ten cords a season, thirty-four years,
    & every joint in my body knows it

by now. But think on this: each waiting round
    has its beauty & surprise: some odd twist
in the grain where the tree stretched or bent
    for light; a sugary pocket of pitch

like dried syrup; a shard of wood the shape
of a bird's head or fish's tail; a blind grub
the color of old parchment, something to toss
to winter wrens that flick & bob

nearby. Even a round with rotten sapwood,
the first two inches laced with termite
tunnels, can hide a center that is solid,
straight-grained, true & bright.

Black Walnut

Our only neighbor to wear a shovel out
through use was Phil, retired engineer
who built bridges in South America before
he moved here to the island & quit

his old life for simple tools & quiet. We joked
about him: "the Phil principle," not quick,
we said, but sure as tides. Deliberate.
When he met you on the road, he tipped his hat,

inclined his head. Old School. A gentleman.
When he was 95 a neighbor found him
planting saplings. He was thin as a rake tine
then, taking a quarter of a shovel load at a time.

Black walnuts, he explained. *But, Phil,
those won't produce for fifty years. You'll
be long gone.* Phil tipped some dirt aside,
leaned on the handle. *What's your point?* he said.

Elk

Solstice, 2018

This was the year the elk swam
to the island, a stray bull turned out
of its Cascade herd & somehow
kicked its way across a mile of saltwater
currents. How could it not love
our unfenced gardens? It browsed
& trampled corn meant for the market
as well as the table, sampled cabbages,
nipped the tender tops of beets. Sightings
were rare, only a patch of hair going
away, a hurried blur in the brush. We knew it
mostly by its tracks & the wreckage
it left. Some farmers slept in their fields.
Flyers appeared on the post office board: *Save
the elk!* Others made jokes about wapiti
burgers. When he found his blueberries
mangled & the lower limbs of apples
& plums torn off in his orchard,
one neighbor leaned a shotgun by his door
& kept watch. It was only a few days
before he saw a giant shape step
into his lower field at dusk.
What he expected when he fired a shot
into the air was panic, but the elk only turned
slightly his way, the pale rack of antlers
warring with the dusky hair
of its neck, before flowing back
into the shadows of the woods:
light dark light dark light

Falcon Watching, Point Disney

What I'd hiked to the highest point
on the island for was to look down
at the hundred-year-old quarry
where sandstone blocks
bound for streets in Everett,
Tacoma, Seattle, were shaped
with special picks until concrete
made the industry moot,
but there it was, a peregrine,
having just caught a pigeon
guillemot in flight,
which was spectacular
enough, but then it drew
a series of loops in the air,
the way a calligrapher
might fall into a flourish
at the end-stroke of a letter,
or a jazz player find & follow
a riff in a sudden pulse
of clear-sighted joy, this
journeyman killer
seized & added a grace note
before settling at the cliff's edge
out of sight behind a patch
of scrub oak, visible
through the leaves as only
brief disturbances of light.

Skeleton

You need to see this!

—Neighbor, working the county road

He has been thinning dead trees
on the county right-of-way across
our west boundary. I heard his saw
& came to find him stepped back
from bucking a cedar that leaned
too far out over the road. At his feet,
under loam & brown curls
of leaves from big leaf maples,
something ivory-colored, broken,
a skull the size of a child's
turned toward the earth, its teeth
half in the dirt, eye socket empty,
a gap in the back of the cranium,
exactly like one I'd seen in a museum
where a sign said the victim was struck
with a stone club. Glimpse of ribs, the bones
of the legs bent at one knee. By the time
he says, *Plastic . . . Halloween . . .*
it's too late: I am thinking of the dream
that keeps coming, me finding a shallow grave
somewhere near home, the crown
of bone just breaking through the duff
like a mushroom & whether I cover it
over & keep it secret or call the sheriff
who would bring with him his dark
questions, no one I love is ever easy
again, no one I love is safe.

IV. Luminous Things

And some will say all sorts of things,
But some mean what they say.

—Robert Frost

Barred Owl

Had it not been for the sound of something
rustling, I might not have looked up
into rain & seen it there, just folding
its wings back into place after shaking
off the wet, its head turned round
staring at me, face a bit heart-
shaped, looking nearly as tired & soaked
as I felt myself. I stood there, wringing
dirty water from my slick leather gloves,
thinking how love comes in & out
of focus like that, a sudden shudder
of sound, a movement of the landscape
that doesn't seem to belong, & there
it is: those eyes that miss nothing, refusing
to be startled, seeing everything clearly.

Wife Descending a Spiral Staircase

I made those stairs myself,
notched each tread into the trunk
of a fir that grew in a long languid
curve for light, so that the stairs are
a spiral. Duchamp had it just
right, how it is all about
time, how she is both at the top
of the stairs, facing me,
& at the bottom where the view
is all her back, orange cat draped
across the shoulders of her winter
robe like a fur cape. She is nineteen
& sixty-two & all the years
between & at each tread I am still
loving her, whether I am here to see
or whether she is there
to be seen.

Boot Jack

Cow manure, garden dirt, pond & pig-
pen mud, woodshed chips, the stink
on the chicken house floor—my grandmother
made this simple aid from two scraps
of barn board & a few re-straightened nails
so she could stick her heel into that cut
shaped like the deep indent of a child's
paper heart & slide off her boots
without help. Wanting to leave
what mess she could on the porch,
my grandmother kept her outside boots
outside. Inside she wore a pair
of sensible canvas shoes. She was the best
person I ever knew in my life before
you. Like her, you know not to buy new
when the old is still sound, & will do.

Keeper

Taken from a box at the end
of January & held under the nose,
brushed slightly with the top
of the upper lip, there is still a scent
of summer light, taste of dew
coating leaves, grass & strands
of spider webs stretched between
branches. You can imagine
the slow buildup of heat & sweet
sugars, the wildest notes of birds
in their morning declarations. But
that first bite tells you
there is also the wisdom of fall
rain, a complexity of taste
that includes wind, the first frost
of the season, the slow descent of
silence, dark nights in the musk
of the storage shed. Even the blemishes—
tiny warts & scales—are sensual
under a rubbing thumb. It seems heavier
in the hand than when picked, more
substantial, asking to be eaten with full
attention, which we gladly give,
savoring it to the core.

Ditch Bouquet, Inis Mór

I am hiking west across the karst
toward the old ring fort on the highest
western cliffs a mile & a quarter
away. It's a gray day: gray skies, a raised
gray sea beyond, gray-feathered birds
gliding above stone blocks the color
of petrified smoke like salt licks shaped
by the slow tongues of rain & wind. From
a long gryke—crack in the limestone—
I pick out crane's bill with its subtle
magenta. At the edge of a shallow
grass bowl comes the blue of harebell,
the purple of tufted vetch. I count seven
shells from sea snails in a clump of eyebright
thrown up by waves in winter, though it's two
hundred sheer feet to the water. Beside a stile
in a rock wall, the spare blooms of thrift,
or sea pink, the muted red of hanging fuchsias
with their multiple clappers. There is a gruff
music in the loose slabs of the clint, a grind
& grunt beneath the feet. Saxifrage—rock breaker—
must hum a slow version of that to itself.
Across a drainage ditch, the white of meadowsweet—
milk curdler—then a scattering of yellow bedstraw
& loosestrife. Last, in a small bite of meadow
by the gate that opens to the main trail rising
to the fort is a dazzling of ox-eye daisies
& a single patch of late-blooming cowslip
offering its deep yellow cups. Imagine me standing
at a sort of altar in the inner ring of stone
walls raised 4,000 years ago on the sea
cliffs. I lay my offering down on the side
that weather does not love, as though
it matters they were gathered & arranged
from all that racked & ragged gray, as though
I actually picked each flower I named.

"Cat's Paw"

i.

When a small gust of wind lightly pats
the water, which sometimes darkens,
for a moment, a small point on the bay,
then spreads out in all directions at once.

ii.

A tool for getting under the head
of a driven nail. It digs in, splinters
the wood, makes the shaft
of the nail scream.

iii.

A sailor's knot, mostly, a hitch
to make two eyes in the bight
of a working rope.

iv.

A dupe, someone made use of
to do a task without knowing
the consequences.

v.

That thing held in your hand
while your thumb rubs the space
between toes, gently, over & over,
while the old cat slows, stops
its labored breathing, lets go of everything
it ever got its claws into.

Barn Cat

The one I remember most
lived in the hay loft or tie-up
of my grandparents' cow
barn, though we could never tell
where for sure. Mostly we saw a blur
the color of floor straw. When he let us
see him, there was always a safe
distance between, & two or three
routes of escape. His left ear was a flap
of skin, a forefoot was missing
toes, but he moved like sunlight
through a board crack. He got fed twice
a day: a few squirts from the dawn
& nighttime milking. It kept him
hungry enough to hunt the mice & rats,
my grandmother said. She'd leave a bowl
of warm water when the cow troughs
froze. She was the only one who could
get near. He'd arch his raggedy-ass back
& rub against those barn boots covered with slick
green manure & purr. Only for her, only for her.

Slugs

We might lift a maple leaf
the size of a dinner plate
& find them tucked in
to one another, half
quote & comma,
slime glistening in the low
light, the color of some
olives, maybe, with lines
of delicate black.

If we tracked their two
iridescent paths back
across the damp duff,
a fallen branch, the shredded
stem of a mushroom,
the charred trunk
of a burned stump
root, we'd find it
impossible to believe
they could have wound up
anywhere but here, ungracious
to wish them anything
but long, slow joy in the beauty
of their meeting.

Anna's

for Sally

"Abiding year around," says one field guide,
no longer a migrator following the bright
names of flowers south, hence this splotch of color
in the front window, drawn by the orange
vision of nasturtiums in a pot on the porch, checking
each wilted blossom before turning to hover
right up against the glass. It's four months
since the last rufous left for an easier life. The
Anna's is tougher, persevering through frost, snow,
rain, & the gray-on-gray times. Very like
you, I often think: *abiding*, "staying on,"
persistent, seeking out every splotch
of color in the bleached, anemic days, as love
enjoins, as strength demands, holding on through lean
months, waiting for light, bearing your own.

Butterflies

Some days her main job seems to be
to welcome back the Red Admiral
as it lights on a leaf of the yellow
forsythia. It is her duty to stop & lean
over to take in how it folds & opens
its wings. Then, too, there is the common
Tiger Swallowtail, which seems to her
entirely uncommon in how it moves
about the boundaries of this clearing
we made so many years ago. If she leaves
the compost bucket unwashed to rescue
a single tattered wing from under the winter
jasmine or the blue flowers of the periwinkle
& then spends a whole afternoon at our round
oak table surrounded by field guides
& tea until she is sure—yes—that it belongs to
a Lorquin's Admiral, or that singular
mark is one of the great cat's eyes
of a Milbert's Tortoiseshell, then she is
simply practicing her true vocation
learning the story behind the blue beads
of the Mourning Cloak, the silver commas
of the Satyr Anglewing, the complex shades
of the Spring Azure, moving through this life
letting her sweet, light attention land
on one luminous thing after another.

2003
Trouble, Mary Baine Campbell
A Place Made of Starlight, Peter Cooley
Taking Down the Angel, Jeff Friedman
Lives of Water, John Hoppenthaler
Imitation of Life, Allison Joseph
Except for One Obscene Brushstroke, Dzvinia Orlowsky
The Mastery Impulse, Ricardo Pau-Llosa
Casino of the Sun, Jerry Williams

2004
The Women Who Loved Elvis All Their Lives, Fleda Brown
The Chronic Liar Buys a Canary, Elizabeth Edwards
Freeways and Aqueducts, James Harms
Prague Winter, Richard Katrovas
Trains in Winter, Jay Meek
Tristimania, Mary Ruefle
Venus Examines Her Breast, Maureen Seaton
Various Orbits, Thom Ward

2005
Things I Can't Tell You, Michael Dennis Browne
Bent to the Earth, Blas Manuel De Luna
Blindsight, Carol Hamilton
Fallen from a Chariot, Kevin Prufer
Needlegrass, Dennis Sampson
Laws of My Nature, Margot Schilpp
Sleeping Woman, Herbert Scott
Renovation, Jeffrey Thomson

2006
Burn the Field, Amy Beeder
The Sadness of Others, Hayan Charara
A Grammar to Waking, Nancy Eimers
Dog Star Delicatessen: New and Selected Poems 1979–2006, Mekeel
    McBride
Shinemaster, Michael McFee

Eastern Mountain Time, Joyce Peseroff
Dragging the Lake, Robert Thomas

2007
Trick Pear, Suzanne Cleary
So I Will Till the Ground, Gregory Djanikian
Black Threads, Jeff Friedman
Drift and Pulse, Kathleen Halme
The Playhouse Near Dark, Elizabeth Holmes
On the Vanishing of Large Creatures, Susan Hutton
One Season Behind, Sarah Rosenblatt
Indeed I Was Pleased with the World, Mary Ruefle
The Situation, John Skoyles

2008
The Grace of Necessity, Samuel Green
After West, James Harms
Anticipate the Coming Reservoir, John Hoppenthaler
Convertible Night, Flurry of Stones, Dzvinia Orlowsky
Parable Hunter, Ricardo Pau-Llosa
The Book of Sleep, Eleanor Stanford

2009
Divine Margins, Peter Cooley
Cultural Studies, Kevin A. González
Dear Apocalypse, K. A. Hays
Warhol-o-rama, Peter Oresick
Cave of the Yellow Volkswagen, Maureen Seaton
Group Portrait from Hell, David Schloss
Birdwatching in Wartime, Jeffrey Thomson

2010
The Diminishing House, Nicky Beer
A World Remembered, T. Alan Broughton
Say Sand, Daniel Coudriet
Knock Knock, Heather Hartley
In the Land We Imagined Ourselves, Jonathan Johnson

Selected Early Poems: 1958-1983, Greg Kuzma
The Other Life: Selected Poems, Herbert Scott
Admission, Jerry Williams

2011
Having a Little Talk with Capital P Poetry, Jim Daniels
Oz, Nancy Eimers
Working in Flour, Jeff Friedman
Scorpio Rising: Selected Poems, Richard Katrovas
The Politics, Benjamin Paloff
Copperhead, Rachel Richardson

2012
Now Make an Altar, Amy Beeder
Still Some Cake, James Cummins
Comet Scar, James Harms
Early Creatures, Native Gods, K. A. Hays
That Was Oasis, Michael McFee
Blue Rust, Joseph Millar
Spitshine, Anne Marie Rooney
Civil Twilight, Margot Schilpp

2013
Oregon, Henry Carlile
Selvage, Donna Johnson
At the Autopsy of Vaslav Nijinksy, Bridget Lowe
Silvertone, Dzvinia Orlowsky
Fibonacci Batman: New & Selected Poems (1991-2011), Maureen Seaton
When We Were Cherished, Eve Shelnutt
The Fortunate Era, Arthur Smith
Birds of the Air, David Yezzi

2014
Night Bus to the Afterlife, Peter Cooley
Alexandria, Jasmine Bailey
Dear Gravity, Gregory Djanikian
Pretenders, Jeff Friedman

How I Went Red, Maggie Glover
All That Might Be Done, Samuel Green
Man, Ricardo Pau-Llosa
The Wingless, Cecilia Llompart

2015
The Octopus Game, Nicky Beer
The Voices, Michael Dennis Browne
Domestic Garden, John Hoppenthaler
We Mammals in Hospitable Times, Jynne Dilling Martin
And His Orchestra, Benjamin Paloff
Know Thyself, Joyce Peseroff
cadabra, Dan Rosenberg
The Long Haul, Vern Rutsala
Bartram's Garden, Eleanor Stanford

2016
Something Sinister, Hayan Charara
The Spokes of Venus, Rebecca Morgan Frank
Adult Swim, Heather Hartley
Swastika into Lotus, Richard Katrovas
The Nomenclature of Small Things, Lynn Pedersen
Hundred-Year Wave, Rachel Richardson
Where Are We in This Story, Sarah Rosenblatt
Inside Job, John Skoyles
Suddenly It's Evening: Selected Poems, John Skoyles

2017
Disappeared, Jasmine V. Bailey
Custody of the Eyes, Kimberly Burwick
Dream of the Gone-From City, Barbara Edelman
Sometimes We're All Living in a Foreign Country, Rebecca Morgan Frank
Rowing with Wings, James Harms
Windthrow, K. A. Hays
We Were Once Here, Michael McFee
Kingdom, Joseph Millar
The Histories, Jason Whitmarsh

2018
World Without Finishing, Peter Cooley
May Is an Island, Jonathan Johnson
The End of Spectacle, Virginia Konchan
Big Windows, Lauren Moseley
Bad Harvest, Dzvinia Orlowsky
The Turning, Ricardo Pau-Llosa
Immortal Village, Kathryn Rhett
No Beautiful, Anne Marie Rooney
Last City, Brian Sneeden
Imaginal Marriage, Eleanor Stanford
Black Sea, David Yezzi

2019
Brightword, Kimberly Burwick
The Complaints, W. S. Di Piero
Ordinary Chaos, Kimberly Kruge
Mad Tiny, Emily Pettit
Afterswarm, Margot Schilpp

2020
Build Me a Boat, Michael Dennis Browne
Sojourners of the In-Between, Gregory Djanikian
The Marksman, Jeff Friedman
Disturbing the Light, Samuel Green
Any God Will Do, Virginia Konchan
My Second Work, Bridget Lowe
Flourish, Dora Malech
Petition, Joyce Peseroff
Take Nothing, Deborah Pope